SERIES 208

In this book we will look at a variety of
environments where animals are able to
thrive – from the marshlands of England
to the outback of Australia.

LADYBIRD BOOKS

UK | USA | Canada | Ireland | Australia
India | New Zealand | South Africa

Ladybird Books is part of the Penguin Random House group of companies
whose addresses can be found at global.penguinrandomhouse.com.

www.penguin.co.uk   www.puffin.co.uk   www.ladybird.co.uk

Penguin
Random House
UK

First published 2020
001

Printed in China

A CIP catalogue record for this book is available from the British Library

ISBN: 978–0–241–41686–0

All correspondence to:
Ladybird Books
Penguin Random House Children's
One Embassy Gardens, New Union Square
5 Nine Elms Lane, London SW8 5DA

MIX
Paper from
responsible sources
FSC® C018179

Animal Habitats

A Ladybird Book

Written by Libby Walden
with zoological consultant, Nick Crumpton

Illustrated by Ayang Cempaka

Woodland

A forest or woodland is an area where trees are the main type of plant. Woodlands are often shaded environments, as the branches of different trees expand and link together to create a natural ceiling, or "canopy". For ground creatures, this shade provides protection during the day and casts shadows at night that help them as they hunt for food.

Black Forest, Germany

The Black Forest in south-west Germany is one of Europe's most famous and established forests. As a forested mountain range, it is home to rivers and streams, protected national parks, untamed woodland, heathland and agricultural land, and as such it hosts a vast variety of animals, birds and insects.

Animal of the Black Forest

The Eurasian lynx is a large wildcat, found in the Black Forest and other forest regions of Europe, Russia and Central Asia. Its thick spotted fur helps it to blend into the wooded environment as it hunts its prey, stalking a variety of animals, from deer to rabbits.

River

Rivers are natural bodies of fresh water that flow along channels in the earth. They travel across countries and pass through different environments, from mountains to meadows and cities to estuaries. As the width, speed and shape of a river changes along its journey, the wildlife that lives in and visits the waterway changes too.

Ganges, Bangladesh and India

The Ganges flows 1,600 miles (2,570 km) from its Himalayan mountain source to the Bay of Bengal. A large number of people live on or near the banks of the river, which means the Ganges has become polluted. This directly affects the river wildlife – for example, the Ganges river dolphin is now considered to be an endangered species.

Animal of the Ganges

Fish-eating gharials live in the freshwater rivers of India and Nepal. Gharials are long-snouted crocodiles that control their body temperature by basking on warm sandy riverbanks and then swimming in cool rivers.

City

Cities are spaces where large numbers of humans live in a small area, and they are home to their own particular type of wildlife. Large volumes of people create a substantial amount of rubbish, and this is considered free food to certain animal and bird species.

New York City, United States of America
The busy streets and loud noises of a city during the day usually stop most animals from coming out of their homes to explore. But at night, when roads and pavements are generally a lot quieter, it is safer for them to roam in search of food, even when the nights are as brightly lit as those in New York.

Animal of New York City
A little brown bat must eat half its body weight every night to stay healthy. As city street lights attract moths and other small insects, these small bats are often found nearby, flying and feasting.

Animal architects

From nests to mounds and hives to lodges, some animal, bird and insect groups, or "species", are incredible builders of amazing and complex structures.

Wild honeybees build their hives in hollow tree trunks, rock crevices and hanging from branches of trees. The worker bees produce and shape natural wax into hexagonal cells that create the layered sheets of honeycomb. These cells are then used to store honey, nectar, pollen and bee larvae.

Towering up to 5 metres (16 ft, 5 in.) high, the mounds of cathedral termites are built using mud, saliva, chewed wood and poo. Despite the impressive height of their mounds, termites actually live beneath the mounds in colonies that can span miles below the surface of the earth.

Not only do beavers build their own homes, known as "lodges", but they also fell trees to create wooden barriers, or "dams". These dams slow down the river and create small, still ponds in which the beavers can safely build their lodges at their leisure.

African mountain gorillas build nests on the ground and in trees. They will rarely sleep in the same nest twice, so they build a new nest every evening, even if it is just a few metres away from the old one.

1. Honeybee hive
2. Termite mound
3. Beaver lodge
4. Gorilla nest

Pond

Ponds are small, shallow bodies of still fresh water. They are either built by humans or created when an underwater spring or rainwater fills a hollow in the ground. As they are isolated pools, the ecosystems within ponds can be very different. Water temperature, cleanliness, plant life and oxygen levels all contribute to the types of animals, fish and organisms that live within a pond.

Ponds are usually self-sufficient, which means they are maintained by the plants and organisms that live in and around the water. Fish and other amphibians produce nutrients and waste that are either absorbed by plants or broken down by bacteria in the water – it's a delicate balancing act.

Pond animal

Also known as a "polliwog", the tadpole is a tiny, wriggly creature that hatches from the eggs of frogs or toads. Its long tail helps it to swim as it looks for plant matter in the water to eat. It takes about fourteen weeks for the tadpole to fully transform into a croaking frog or toad.

Tropical rainforest

A tropical rainforest is a natural environment of tall trees that experiences a high level of rainfall every year. Tropical rainforests grow in areas that sit along the equator, and because of this their warm climate and access to sunshine lasts all year round. Plants thrive in this environment, and it is estimated that two-thirds of all plant species grow in the rainforests of the world.

Amazon Rainforest, South America
The trees, shrubs and foliage within a tropical rainforest, such as the Amazon, grow naturally in four clear levels, or "layers" – the emergent, canopy, understory and forest floor. The majority of rainforest wildlife lives above ground in the canopy. Here, creatures are safe from land-based predators and have access to the fruits and nuts of the forest trees.

Animal of the Amazon Rainforest
The emerald tree boa spends almost all of its life in the branches of the rainforest canopy. As a nocturnal creature, the boa will rest during the day, coiled on a branch, before using its strong tail to move and hunt at night.

Polar habitats

There are lands of ice and snow at the points furthest north and south of the globe. The extreme conditions and cold temperatures of the Arctic and Antarctic limit the type of wildlife that is able to survive in these areas. For example, as plants are unable to grow successfully on these plains, animals that live in polar regions often rely on the availability of meat or fish for food.

Ross Ice Shelf, Antarctica

The largest platform of ice in Antarctica is the Ross Ice Shelf. Sitting on the coast of the continent, it is the world's biggest area of floating ice and is hundreds of metres thick. Most of it is hidden underwater, and animals that live on or around the ice usually have to live above and below the surface to survive.

Animal of the Ross Ice Shelf

The smallest species of penguin in the Antarctic is the Adélie. Its main food source is krill, so it has to enter the icy waters to hunt. Adélies can dive to depths of 150 metres (492 ft) and hold their breath underwater for up to six minutes.

Rock pool

Rock pools, or "tide pools", are found along rocky coastlines around the world. When the tide is high, these pools are hidden underwater as part of the rocky seabed. But once the tide goes out, they become small natural aquariums that host a variety of ocean plants and creatures, giving them a place to survive between tides.

Rock pools are not fixed environments. They are affected by the tide every day. Once the tide is high enough to cover the pool, its salty water is refreshed, and creatures can come and go between the pool and the open ocean. The wildlife within a rock pool depends on the pool's size, depth, temperature, salt content and exposure to light.

Rock pool animal
The butterfish is a small fish without scales that feeds in shallow waters on hermit crabs and marine worms. It is able to breathe air through its gills, which helps it to survive if it gets stranded in a rock pool during low tide.

Nest builders

A nest is a structure commonly associated with birds. It is a place where eggs are laid and chicks are fed, but, much like the different styles, sizes and shapes of human houses, not all birds' nests look the same.

The outer layer of the ovenbird's dome-shaped nest is covered in leaves and small sticks to help it blend into the leaf litter on the ground.

Female flamingos lay eggs in a shallow dip on the top of their mound nests. The parents then take it in turns to sit on the egg to keep it warm.

Pairs of barn swallows build their cup-shaped nests together, using mud and grass to form the basic shape.

The bald eagle reuses its platform nest, known as an "aerie", every year, returning to spruce it up with new material at the start of the nesting season.

The great spotted woodpecker digs its own cavity-shaped nest by using its beak to drill holes into tree trunks.

Most weavers build pendant-shaped nests that hang from branches, with an entrance at the base or side to protect against invading predators.

1. Dome nest
2. Mound nest
3. Cup nest
4. Platform nest
5. Cavity nest
6. Pendant nest

Mountain Tundra

"Alpine tundra" is the name given to the rocky area above the treeline on a mountainside. Trees cannot grow on this part of the mountain due to the high elevation and cold temperatures, so the vegetation in these areas is mainly hardier grasses and shrubs.

Rocky Mountain Range, North America
All alpine tundras, including those found at the top of the Rocky Mountains, are unique. They experience difficult environmental conditions under extreme weather and limited seasonal changes. As such, the animals and birds that live here are as tough and hardy as the plants.

Animal of the Rocky Mountain Range
The North American bighorn sheep is known for its large, curled horns and special hooves that help it to scale the rocky terrain. The rough bottoms of the hooves add grip, and the split design of each hoof helps with balance.

Tropical Savannah

As environments, the tropical and subtropical savannahs are often categorized by the animals that wander across their vast grasslands. A savannah is a mix of woodland and open plains that is subject to dry conditions, a single season of rainfall and the threat of dry-season wildfires.

Serengeti, Tanzania

In Africa, the Serengeti is an enormous ecosystem in which the climate, weather patterns and wildlife are believed to have remained the same for as long as it has existed. Its name comes from the Maasai word *siringet* meaning "endless plains", and this vast environment supports more than 30 species of large mammal and 500 species of bird.

Animal of the Serengeti

The fastest land mammal is the African cheetah. As it darts towards its prey, the cheetah uses its long tail to balance its weight so it can safely race across the Serengeti at speeds of up to 60 miles (97 km) per hour.

Marshland

An area of land that either lies below sea level or is fed by a water source and supports grasses, rushes and reeds is known as a "marsh". Water covers marshland for long periods of time, making it home to both aquatic and semiaquatic wildlife, as well as a large variety of birds. Marshes can also be found by lakes and streams, where the ground changes from water to solid land.

Thorpe Marshes, England

Norfolk's Thorpe Marshes is a flower rich marshland that borders the River Yare and the lake of Whitlingham Great Broad. As it sits between two bodies of water, the land often floods and is home to a variety of waterbirds, mammals and the rare Norfolk hawker dragonfly.

Animal of the Thorpe Marshes

The Chinese water deer is not a native species, but it has thrived in the Norfolk marshlands. It feasts on the herbs and grasses of the reed bed, and its sharp sense of smell means that it can quickly escape when it senses danger.

Coral reef

Coral reefs are underwater habitats formed by groups, or "colonies", of a plant-like animal called coral. They mostly form in warm, shallow parts of the ocean and provide a home for at least 25 per cent of all marine life. The species of coral that build reefs are known as "hard" or "hermatypic" corals. They create a stable ecosystem because they develop a strong exoskeleton on the outside of their soft bodies using chemicals from the seawater.

The Great Barrier Reef, Australia

The world's largest coral reef is the Great Barrier Reef, which is off the coast of Queensland, Australia. Stretching over 1,200 miles (1,931 km), this natural wonder is estimated to be approximately 20,000 years old and can be seen from space. It is home to a hugely diverse range of creatures, including vulnerable and endangered species.

Animal of the Great Barrier Reef

The spotted clown nudibranch, or "sea slug", lives in warm, shallow reefs in Australia and New Zealand. The two "horns" on the top of its head are actually tentacles that help the nudibranch with touch, taste and smell. It is often found living on sea sponges, which are also its main food source.

Deep underground

Some creatures live underground. The dark and damp conditions below the earth's surface create warm and, mostly, secure homes.

The muscular shoulders, short legs and curved claws of the South African golden mole help it to "swim" through sandy earth. Its webbed hind legs clear the debris it leaves behind.

The common earthworm feasts on decomposing plant materials. It then breaks down the nutrients and returns them to the soil. Gardeners love earthworms, as they improve the soil while they tunnel through the earth.

Magellanic penguins burrow under rocks and bushes to create safe places to lay their eggs. The fluffy grey chicks stay underground in the nest until they are old enough to go to sea and hunt.

The tunnels and chambers dug by European badgers are known as "setts". These networks are usually large enough to house fifteen or more badgers.

Unlike most spiders, the trapdoor spider lives in an underground burrow with a hinged door at the entrance. It waits behind the camouflaged door until it detects prey passing by – then the spider leaps out to catch it!

1. Golden mole
2. Common earthworm
3. Magellanic penguin
4. European badger
5. Trapdoor spider

Meadow

Meadows are grass fields that are grown by farmers for the purpose of harvesting hay. However, the term has also come to mean any field that is naturally or intentionally growing wild. Tall grasses provide structure and shelter for smaller habitats within a meadow, which are havens for insects and minibeasts.

The quality and type of soil in a meadow determines the types of flowers and insects that live there. For example, wetter or chalkier soils are suited to flowers that attract more butterflies, and soil with a high acid content might increase grass growth and encourage moths and beetles to the area.

Meadow animal

The meadow grasshopper is found throughout the summer in damp, overgrown meadows across Europe and Asia. Its green, striped body blends into the grassy environment. The smaller male meadow grasshopper tries to attract females by rubbing its leg against its wing to create a "song".

Lowland forest

Lowland forests are very similar to rainforests, as they experience warm temperatures, high levels of rainfall and humidity, and year-round plant growth. Trees and plants grow in layers and create a variety of smaller microhabitats within lowland forests, which allows for a rich ecosystem.

Andohahela National Park, Madagascar

The tropical lowland forests of Madagascar make up a complex environment with dense vegetation and a high number of animal and insect species. This is because, millions of years ago, the island was connected to both Africa and India. As a result, the wildlife is hugely diverse and contains species that are only found in Madagascar.

Animal of the Andohahela National Park

The ring-tailed lemur is only found in the lowland forests of the African island of Madagascar. It lives in groups, or "troops", above the ground. The lemur does not use its striking black-and-white tail for grip when climbing, but instead covers it in natural scents to waft at rival lemurs.

Open ocean

More than 70 per cent of the earth's surface is covered in water, and half of that is open ocean. This makes the open ocean the largest ecosystem on earth. The term "open ocean" refers to the oceanic water that is above the seabed and beyond the coastline. It is a vast and unpredictable habitat – some areas are filled with life, and others appear totally lifeless.

Only a relatively small percentage of marine species live in the open ocean, but it is home to some of the most amazing and recognizable sea creatures, including the largest animal on the planet – the blue whale.

Ocean animal

The common thresher, or fox, shark is known for its enormous tail fin, which is just as dangerous to prey as its rows of sharp teeth. It will whip its long tail at schools of fish, such as herring or mackerel, to break them up and injure multiple fish at a time – this makes it easier for the shark to hunt.

Mangrove

A mangrove is a coastal ecosystem that is found in and around tropical lagoons, islands and estuaries (the place where rivers meet the ocean). It is made up of mangrove trees. These trees are able to grow in saltwater and so thrive along the shoreline. The roots of these trees create shelter for a large variety of aquatic animals, as they break down the force of the tide, and so protect infant fish.

The Sundarbans, Bangladesh

The Bangladesh Sundarbans is a mangrove forest that grows where three main rivers meet the ocean. Made up of waterways, mudflats and saltwater-tolerant mangrove trees, it is a complex river network that supports over 250 bird species and many endangered animals, including the Royal Bengal tiger, olive ridley turtle and the water monitor lizard.

Animal of the Sundarbans

The mudskipper is one of the few species of fish that is able to live outside of the water. It uses its strong front fins to drag itself over the mud of swamps and river mouths, skipping and crawling across land to feed on crabs. It survives by breathing through its gills and skin while on land.

Outback

The outback is the vast expanse of dry land in the middle of Australia. This enormous space spans 2.5 million square miles (6.5 million square km), and experiences several extreme climates, including freezing winters, droughts and high levels of humidity and rainfall.

Flinders Ranges, Australia
Much of the land in the outback is described as "arid" or "semi-arid", which means it is dry and scorched. The Flinders Ranges is the largest mountain range in South Australia and also part of a stony desert region. As such, the area is full of well-adapted, robust wildlife that is able to cope well with the harsh surroundings.

Animal of the Flinders Ranges
The Australian emu is the second-tallest bird on the planet, following the ostrich. Although it needs to drink water every day, this flightless bird can survive in the dry outback for several days without food. It stores fat in its body that it can burn for energy until it finds insects or plants to eat.

A Ladybird Book

collectable books for curious kids

What to Look For in Spring

9780241416181

What to Look For in Summer

9780241416204

What to Look For in Autumn

9780241416167

What to Look For in Winter

9780241416228

SERIES 205

Baby Animals

9780241416907

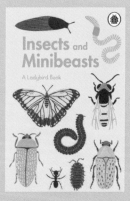

Insects and Minibeasts

9780241417034

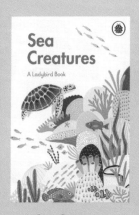

Sea Creatures

9780241417072

Trees

9780241417218

SERIES 208

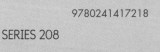